SAFE HO

Safe Home

MÍCHEÁL MCCANN

Be well,

Mícheál McCann

Green Bottle Press

First published in 2020
by Green Bottle Press
83 Grove Avenue
London N10 2AL
www.greenbottlepress.com

Cover design by Økvik Design
Cover image from Garden World Images
Typeset by CB editions, London
Printed in England by Imprint Digital, Exeter EX5 5HY

ISBN 978-1-910804-19-3

for Des, i.m., and for Sinéad, pure light

ACKNOWLEDGEMENTS

Thanks are due to the editors of the following journals in which some of these poems appeared: Eavan and Colette (*Poetry Ireland Review*), Claire, Eimear and Laura (*Banshee Lit*), Manuela and Stephen (*The Lifeboat*), and Eoin, Una and Louise (*The Cormorant*). A deep bow of appreciation.

I'm grateful for the time spent in the company of wonderful teachers and mentors, and the conversations. Indescribable thank-yous to Stephen Sexton, Sinéad Morrissey, Leontia Flynn, Paul Maddern, Nick Laird and Ciaran Carson.

Because poems happen out of life as well as lessons, I would be remiss to not thank the people who have shaped my thinking and seeing, directly and indirectly, over the past few years: Hilary Copeland / Alison Garden / Catherine Gander (my first true teacher) / Stefanie Lehner / Olivia Fitzsimmons / Bethany Ashley / Philip McGowan / Eli Davies / Jan Carson / Kelsie Donnelly / Patrick Keane / Gail McConnell / Ellen Orchard / Milena Williamson / Laura Kennedy (my gladiator) / Nidhi Zak/Aria Eipe / Evelyn Wilson (for always knowing) / Kelly O'Brien.

Particular glimmering thanks to Dawn 'GAF' Watson and Charles Lang. What a happy office.

Thank you to my editor Jennifer Grigg, for her expertise and kindness, and the loudest thank you to Mark Doty and Miriam Gamble, heroes, for lending their words to describe this pamphlet of poems.

I am grateful to the Arts Council of Northern Ireland for an ACES Award toward the completion of these poems, and am deeply grateful to know the most-committed supporter of new writing in NI, Damian Smyth.

For my parents, for everything, for sticking with me and bringing me back.
For my red-head brother, Conor. A lot of those poems are in pure celebration of you.
For Andrew, with my love, and for all the talking.

sanctuary was still sanctuary
except more so, with the inside
holding flickeringly, and the
outside clamouring in.

– Sinéad Morrissey

Contents

Études

I'll go to concerts in the Ulster Hall
a few times a year to see the violin soloists.
My friends think that
this is because I want to learn
fingerboard electric dashes of
the Shostakovich or the Barber
– nothing so heroic –
I go in the hope that something goes
wrong. The gold-plated E string
snapping mid-cadenza. An earring
slipping off, bouncing on the chin rest
then the floor *pop pop . . . Bang*

– how these people can deal with disaster
at a moment's notice:

the string snapping in the middle
of a mournful B section of something
Tchaik-like

could I learn this, this coping?

2 Photograph of Hallé Orchestra, 1901

A stage full of coat tails and
cocks between all of their legs
nestled like trapdoor spiders
but one harpist, renowned
for her *dexterous*, impossibly
agile fingers, and *sensitive,
emotive playing.*

3 *Urstudien*

The central heating system
growls – no – rumbles
The house going to sleep my mother would say

and I am pressing and lifting
all four fingers in different chord
patterns to strengthen the muscles in my fingers

but I am struggling to anchor
my three fingers on intervals
while the index is active with *elastic surety*.

A strange drum-like singing
– my bow unsheathed –
as I'm trying to be quiet. My fingers collapse

under the pressure I place
on them, rightly. The washing
machine burps. We duet into the night.

4 Amateur Prayer

I pick up my violin that wishes it remained a forest.
On a Sunday that is milky with undammed rain I watch

the soloists – so giant I decorate their ankles with
iron lanterns, that my children will remember them –

execute this piece precisely. I struggle to write
the word *perfectly*, unsure what it looks like. Content

is a word I'm prioritising as my fingers clump
like cheese over chords I cannot play. Sing a song.

Play, she'll say,
and toast our amateurism. It's the only thing we have left.

Babel, just before; just after

Then I had no fair ringlets budding
from my flower bed chest. My father
returned from the site each night
bare-chested – eyes hooded, his hand
reaching forward as I hand him the can
and he laughs in bat-disturbing booms
and he's been wearing a dust-sheet
as a cape this entire time! *Let's fly!* He said and
he washes his hands in watery vinegar.
The mortar goodbyes into the running
water. I wasn't allowed to watch him work,
higher and higher, and even my owl friend
stopped circling after long. While he worked:
the washing, damp; the postcard, unsent;
the wildflowers, everywhere! Oh, colour . . .

I visit my father in a dream: I fidget
at the tower base. He is strong, sure,
and never tires. He places bricks like me
into bed and he won't stop reaching,
sweaty and flower-crowned, until he arrives
at the pale, empty moon: satisfied.

Then the bricks fell from the sky sounding
like *fire oh fire oh plunge my eyes*
or maybe *incredible head trauma?*
and my da watches his work: weeping stars,
wondering what I'd think, or newly, who I was becoming.
Our words remained the same, but
I grew confused in my greenery when daddy
offered how to emulsify the wall for painting
when I asked him about PrEP
when I asked how to love
when they have the same.
My da would shout for something
from the garage, but the smell
of paper distracted me.
A drill? A beer? A hand
pressed into daddy's hand? My voice
to him, the same indistinct rumble as his
through the sad veins of the house. Two voices
one low, one deepening:
hugging the walls, vibrating for help.

Peadar's

Better they will never warm me, though they must
Light several Winters' fires. Before they are done
– Edward Thomas

Christmas was light-sore and slipping away
and Derry was ready for the darkened room.

The traditional music pub heavy with flags
-for-ceiling recently(ish) replaced a grisaille,

rectangle panel with a shout of a rainbow.
If the banjo player is leading this quintet

the beardy, pint-kissed dancers conduct.
Exerted with holding the whole thing

together, his neck is murrey, full of blood.
Everyone cheers when *Fairytale* starts.

Even the bartenders stop. Teeth full of milk.
There are more teeth, more smiles than ways

to feasibly escape. Brace, brace. A bar-wide
survey has everyone's lips bared for *f* anfare,

and he says it around a grin. They proclaim it!
The wind hurries in. No one hears last orders.

Ignorance (The Country Farm)

after Lloyd Schwartz

The air outside smelling of milk and fresh bread.

A sudden smell of manure.

The most brittle breeze.

The yard patrolled by two or three dogs (one with bronze fur – bronze!).

The dog understanding a young boy growing old on the inside bit.

Blue finches, particularly how they flick their heads like people trying to shake off a sad day.

How the sky never is quite right until he wakes.

Scott (the dog) dreaming of being abandoned with his brown eyes glassy and open.

A friend's father – masculine in anger – walks so firmly an unsure face fills with the promise of blood.

A quad bike rip-roaring awake.

A boy with blonde hair dreams a door closed hard, the unforgiving rain sheeting the wood of the door.

The yellow rectangle tags hanging from the sheep's ear look like glamorous earrings he'll say.

The living room, aching with aged, ruffled leather, falling silent.

The wildflowers (blue-eyed grass, dark-red helleborine, butterwort) growing from various shaped and sized pots along the track.

The largest pot: terracotta slate.

An errant stone throw lacerates a vein of the pot, some soil and roots spill down – brown, damp waterfall –

Strangers – children – playing fort/da in view of the draughty window.

Agitated hay fever.

The quad being refilled. Drink up!

The grasp of four feet to exposed attic beams, no, balance beams (sawdust as silent and glinting in the air as this unexplained erection)

A far-off crying; animal or human, him or? Dunno.

Baking bread with an aunt while the other boys bend rough hands over spade handles.

Picking speckled eggs – hens clucking – felt like acceptance.

Outside resplendent in cow song; far off honks; geese making trouble; foxes keening; wind whistling off of the grass.

Silence is fiction (Photographs are still windows.)

The sow is giving birth all through the star-peppered night.

Drying whitewash stubbornly staining under nails and pale yellow dungarees; *fuck sake* someone roars with a smile you can hear.

A warm bed. You are seven.

A hand drops from the bunk above you, reaching down. The hand needs a hand.

The sun, a horizon off, stretches itself.

Man & Woman

The bus resigns to leave its Belfast bed, burdened
    by pages and appointments
with a familiar given-up sigh as my eyes come
    to a pair on the platform
hugging all Jack and Rose soft-dry-hump-like,
    sparkling and safe and dry.
A plague of pigeons watch via Galilean binoculars.
    I hate them. How *carelessly* they . . .

A woman with dark jewels presses her form against
    his front: firm, holding, terrifying.
No – this rage-fired view isn't fair. I want this.
    The theatre of half-missed kisses
in the pain of the grey hour outside the Europa.
    Not anticipating the glimmer of *fags*,
or the tight-collared relative eyeing a grazing tongue
    as they smell for some mint tea.

Why garden? – bulbs full of light, trouble – when
    this safe home could be a bus station,
the concert line, walking the longest bridge in town.
    But the quiet garden. Ours alone.
We develop, us lucky many, a new way of things.
    A new dramatic theory. Quiet; there.
A tree leans to the plainsong of two similar-sized,
    sure hands. I lower a book

on optimism onto my groin and call him – phone stalls –
    call his name. Laugh at the wind, hold me closed a while,
&

Edward Hopper: *Early Sunday Morning, 1939*

after, for Ciaran Carson

opal and shallow sea
marrying in the sky

good morning they say
street below stirring

gap of one sheer
drape to the next

shaped like a body
painted dark

the shops yawn
still bleary

no coffee
in sight

you notice what
the shadows do

while we fume
at the queue

to get our moustache
taken in

snip snip
scratch

you
smirking man

sketching the waiting
room in pencil

oily grease on boards
or a gleam

gold tooth
joke you don't get yet

muggy outside
on seventh

the avenue empty
bar those

awake this early
finding time

Fried Egg Sandwich

Ellen, the night has been at the unknocked door
since you left, and isn't going away despite my loud reading
about somewhere – anywhere – else.

Your face has become acquainted with my worn, pocked
    phone screen:
sanctuary spilling out. Let us be courageous, you'd say.

Birdsong pecks through my rudimentary speaker and whiskers
of garnet flowers bob behind you. I'm there, and
never have been there.

I've begun to say *man* when I mention a person
or conclude a tough day, breathing out quietly.

I've internalised how you speak
(we live our love)
and take you with me as I unlock the front door

to find a carton of fresh eggs. Oh man, I'll say
as one breaks – it: laughing – over my jorts. Oh man, I'll say
as an afternoon rain comes on over my yard.

And if it blesses yours too, that you have that huge parka,
that Joni is playing from the radio inside so faintly
she could be confused for hope.

The Hopes

after Colette Bryce

The wings reach out
smooth as stilling water

slicing the air like
carrots. The night at height

makes home glittery; the garden
below an inverted sky.

Darkness and then!
ranges of amber, waving flowers.

A thin fleece of cirrus
duvets Derry. You saved us.

Hook-Up

rural Donegal

Lonely people waking
to scroll through Grindr
at 1:38am of a Wednesday.
The nearest Gay™ is 7 km away
and if I had to be brutally honest

like a hesitant carpenter, Norway somewhere,
wary of a wood-shortage in his perilous future,
I don't want the split-second warm
unpleasant-later feeling of his saliva
marking my dick like a dog against a tree.

I want to reach around
the green circle (online now!)
that lets me know they're the same as me:
awake, scrolling down like Croft
through a papyrus looking

for the right inscription.
And then our hands can reach,
join in the middle somewhere
across this pitch-black Donegal landscape,
and we wouldn't touch in the moonlight

as mystery insects buzz
by the fence posts, and ewes rest
under trees: content instead to watch new lambs
make their way through the darkness
to their mothers, in complete, holy silence.

Letter from the Living

The Glenshane opened all bookish and smiling
into a muckily dark sky, ornamented in stars.
The silver car that takes petrol is puffering up
the mountain. Meridian water kisses apart
the grass, the sky a canvas: paradise of grammar.

I'm seeing this clockwork as some sallow poem and
Fox! It's jaw parted in a twisted grin, preparing
the inside joke only it and its lover would get
when the silver car that took petrol parted
its ribcage from its chest – the sharp sting

of attention – and no one to see but me.
Lying on its bleeding back, jaw still snapped wide
as though drawing breath from painful laughter.
Eyes that say nothing except *who have I left
behind.* A chest ruptured like grape skin, eyes

say *Off to get some milk, heart still beating
my kids still sleeping I want to go be happy.*
The silver car drove on eventually. Spitting
petrol like tears: the petroleum slick promising
iridescence but no light falls up here. Not now.

The William Mannell

The ten metres you can see is the unbearable part
   I argue At least above water you'd see things coming
      knowing I'm wrong knowing sight is no pal in a knife fight.

The real trouble is being bone dry and the Man of War
   somehow sneaks up on you and for no reason your form
      just full of light calls Come in to the overly motherly jellyfish.

Your diving stopped while I was still swimming, after
   a fashion, but your eyes lit like rose glass recounting
      how brilliantly fired a wreck looked in the failing summer.

Hull plates and decking have rotted into the sand
   so only rusted ribs, framework, mooring bollards resist
      your body – neoprene-smooth – entry to Atlantis.

You descend slowly from a world of clamour into one
   of deep fruiting silence. The late afternoon uncovers the furore
      of red and purpling anemones; dead man's fingers waving back.

In the warm-blue darkness of the hull the silty floor
   is alive with lost jewels scintillating slinking past each other
      on the hull floor: light peeks from rotted holes above your head.

As you slow to a still float, a theatre of silt takes its turn:
   head pivoting wing to wing. This place, like Earth, but flipped.
      I smell your father smoking in the captain's plush cabin. Door?
         locked.

And the giant probably blue lobster you heard rumours
   about is nowhere to be seen or heard *clack clack snapping*
      but you do see two claws reaching kindly from a hole in the wall.

A dinner plate of a crab, fallen in when it was smaller, sprightly,
    nooked, and grew and grew too grand. In its trapped rest it felt
        like God. Now it has outgrown its haven as you have this
            adrenaline fix

and you rise to the surface despite your limbs' nitrogen ache.
    Do you mourn the passing of your underworld? I'm so sorry
        it was the first way I made things difficult. I suppose this poem

is me trying to resurrect the beneath. You say one pitch night
    that you might take the notion to dive again and I am haunted
        in sleep by purple waves broiling with talk. And you're smiling:

coul-pinched face, your suited feet first break the beach waves.
    A diving knife in one hand, the other slashed from a sharp,
        wise coral. You're on the wood boat with both bone-hilt oars
            accounted for.

The last thing my eyes remember before I surface
    into the unbearable: a flat, strong hand, pointed to me.
        Rising up and down, meaning *Stay calm. I'll be okay*

Leaving London for Belfast

for Andrew

Rather be parochial
than suitcase-weary
and tie-bonded
and slow to laugh
and desperate
to walk the opposite direction,
quickly . . .

Rather be coastal
than coughing,
slow in our going
than quiet with wanting.
Bless this plane, carrying
us over what we cannot swim.

My tired thighs hear
where we're going over the tannoy
and I can hear Jo Stafford
smiling as she sings. I missed you.
I hoak for a life vest under my seat
to realise I was wearing it all along.

The Man with His Child in His Eyes

Oh some December when I was small, wavy: when things
might only hurt for a while. Derry was lit and springy.
    Street lights were rung round

by wind-strong tinsel. The city may have been wrapped
in heating filaments keeping everything flirting
    with boiling.

A not-so-bad winter has ordained the spired city
with more palatable discontents: finance, the sadness
    of Christmas, youth waning.

I was four and knew even then that what I needed
was not words or money, so I took the Yellow Mouse
    with Red Cheeks and ran!

from the shop. My father was 'cross' and 'embarrassed',
and spent the walk back to the car trying to conceal the
    cheek-slashing grin as some furrowed grimace.

Driving back along the Foyle, the City of Spires let us go.
An innocent shoplifter and his accomplice: the Robin
    still attempting the effacing

of a freckle-stretching smile: as precious as Movillian
sea glass, beer bottle bottoms transformed in the happy carnage
    of the sea. Charmed by boldness.

Wee man: he loves bold bastards. Singular bastard. Mind
this as you go. Daddy's stepping thigh-deep into the Lackagh
    and his waders

catch Donegal rubies, or are they salmon roe? in the water
    that runs like your heart.

Apology

Sleep is not answering the phone
while the directors of our terrain

(we imagine them as coyotes
in carrot-coloured pant-suits)

ignore the line than runs red-hot
along the gated field by our house.

You, Fire Boy, lavish inside: the day's
sun knocks against your drawn curtain

and from the outside your room
flashes with strobe-bang! brilliance.

An Irish heat distorts the pavement
but fear not, you are building a city.

This room you game in. Your bolthole
was mine long ago but I lost the deed,

keep it, and keep your hands moulded
around what allows control of your world.

When I roar about reading or wild herbs
I only envy this wonderful new world

you craft, its crystal blue water, how
the villagers shout *Hail!* to everyone...

This world, built block by grassy block:
gold-brown truffles; fish leap the river.

Your brow is smooth, no tell-tale furrow.
I pull the curtain tighter, settle to watch.

Brother

where have you
    gone my pal
        in a bang of fire and hair
and wearing and tearing
    your stare is playing
        hide and seek
and is skilled but
    i find it i always will
        and even though
i am hiding from you
    after a fashion
        half behind the oak tree
out the back in Culdaff
    the sea's there!
        and the tire!
i am with my dear friend
    so you think
        and here is this for you
    to find sometime: me
        clumsy in things
but always here-abouts
    even when i am not
        even when we leave toothpaste
opened and oozy even when
    we drive our ma to distraction
        even when you don't know the truth
            yet
    find me here. i'll stay until then.
        will be by the water.

Prayer

Looking down
absently into
a train table
like it'll tell me—
a phone's black mirror
lets downcast eyes
see sheep-gutty clouds
in an August sky
in the glass
of a locked phone.
Turning upward
to the real thing
my eyes
are lit.